MW00785173

TURNOVER FILES

TURNOVER FILES

A NAVY MAN'S JOURNEY

NANA BONSU

Nana Bonsu

This book is dedicated to my Family, Friends, and Service Members

I

Table of Contents

II

Decisions

Written By
Nana Bonsu

Disclaimer

The views presented are those of the author, and do not necessarily represent the views of the Navy or DoD.

DECISIONS

"My detailer lied to me," is usually what service members say about how they joined the military. In my case, my detailer didn't lie to me, he just didn't give me the right information to succeed in the United States Navy.

My journey began while contemplating how to travel the world and earn money to attend college. I still remember sitting outside on a bench at my high school weeks before graduation, trying to figure things out. Whatever the plan, I did not want to burden my parents, who were already stressed paying for my older brother's college tuition.

While thinking, a Navy recruiter approached me and asked about my intentions after high school. Since I had no real answer, he offered the Navy as an option. It seemed like a win-win at the time. Travel the world and receive the Montgomery G.I. Bill to use as funding for college. One important message he shared was for me to focus on my career and not on distractions, such as parties and girls. Rather, he encouraged me to join the Navy to learn a skill set and get an education. He said everything else I wanted would fall in place on its own.

At the time, I was still considered a minor when I made up my mind to join the Navy, which meant I had to get approval from my parents to sign my life away. I knew my mother would not agree, coming from a traditional West African family. And I was unsure about what my father's response would be. But I hoped it would make him proud to know his son was making a choice to serve the country.

Of course, my mother cried and pleaded with me not to join the military, but I stood firm behind my decision. My father turned out to be more supportive than I thought. I could tell it gave him a sense of pride that I was becoming a man of my own.

If I could encourage anyone reading this, my first advice would be to stand by your decisions.

BOOT CAMP

Leaving for boot camp was exciting for me because it was my first time traveling to another state. I left with a group of guys from the Great State of Texas and we were all under the impression that we would stay together throughout the boot camp process. We were wrong. The initial excitement turned into anxiety, confusion, and fear of the unknown.

I remember arriving in the Chicago O'Hare Airport late at night. We were then met by a uniformed Recruit Division Commander, who escorted us into a bus full of other boot camp recruits. All I could think about was, "What the heck did I sign up for?" My stomach was in knots. I wasn't prepared for all the screaming and yelling from all sides.

After a couple of days getting processed through the system, I was surprised to learn I could have arrived at boot camp with the rank of E-3 rank instead of E-1. I also could have received an enlistment bonus, which was never mentioned by my recruiter. Nonetheless, this gave me the motivation to do my best to advance in rank and set myself up for success.

LEARNING CURVE

At boot camp, I learned about different cultures and cities within the United States. I met people from rough neighborhoods, with military backgrounds, and some with unique accents. There were people in boot camp because they were ordered by a judge to either serve in the military or go to prison. We were a wild bunch.

I've never been to jail or prison, but boot camp was what I imagined it to be. For example, we had to shower together, had a time limit to eat, and slept with one eye open. We literally woke up at various times early in the morning to make up our racks within a set amount of time. Some veterans believe living in such austere conditions builds character, but it only made us anxious and envy one another.

For instance, some people were able to make their racks in record time while others couldn't. The latter paid the price through extraneous workout activities. As a result, those who were not fast enough to make their racks would bully those who did. Over time, we learned how to help each other and work as a team.

Overall, the boot camp experience was unique and challenging. I learned to value people's differences. I also learned to help people when possible. The Recruit Division Commanders also left us with important jewels that resonated throughout my military career, such as DO NOT date co-workers in the Navy, and to keep your spouse away from other military spouses. Disclaimer: I am not endorsing that advice, but I have personally witnessed a slew of Sailoron-Sailor relationships and they were very complicated and ended badly. Conversely, some rose above the drama and had great relationships-- GREAT! Again, I'm neutral on this topic.

CHOOSE YOUR RATE, CHOOSE YOUR FATE

During boot camp, we had a day dedicated to choosing our rating in the Navy. Choosing a rate was basically selecting a job in the Navy. We had seconds to decide what we were interested in doing. Luckily, I expressed to my recruiter before I left that I was interested in anything related to business accounting. Thus, he suggested the Disbursing Clerk (DK) rate, which dealt with payroll. The recruiter also mentioned the Storekeeper (SK) rate, which dealt with supply chain management and financials. In the end, I decided to become an SK because it sounded cooler to be called an SK rather than a DK. Heck, I didn't want anyone to make fun of me by calling me a "dick," because that is what I would have called someone with those abbreviated letters.

Going back to boot camp, some of us already had rates assigned before boot camp. However, we individually had to verify if we still wanted our rating; if not, we were reassigned a rate. Those who were undecided or without a rate were given the rate as an undesignated seaman or undesignated airman. Honestly, I didn't understand much of the rating discussions aside from the fact that we all had a job to perform to make the Navy better as a whole.

After graduating from boot camp, most of us with ratings departed to various A-Schools to learn our jobs. But those who were undesignated were given airline tickets straight to the fleet to report to their commands aboard ships and air stations. Choose your rate, choose your fate.

A-SCHOOL

Meridian, Mississippi is the A-School location for Navy Storekeepers. That place was terrible. Coming from city life, my impression of Mississippi was slow and country. It didn't help that all that I knew of Mississippi was its contribution to segregation and racism. I was not thrilled to be there.

After we arrived at the training base, I was told by one of the A-School students on duty to go to my room and change out of my uniform quickly. He told me to relax and enjoy my freedom. Our rooms were set up like college dorms. We had four rooms and one common living room area for eight people to share. It felt like a movie scene where a person gets out of prison and finally has a chance to experience the world. I had missed out on so much and was eager to enjoy my freedom.

The first order of business was to unpack my sea bag and wear the civilian clothes I put away in boot camp. Fashion had changed, so we made a run to the mall to buy new shoes and clothes. I also recall wanting to buy a necklace for my mom as a "*Thank You*" gesture. The sharks at the mall saw me coming a mile away and convinced me to buy jewelry at a high-interest rate. In hindsight, it was a bad purchase. But the experience taught me to be more cognizant about making better business decisions, especially with purchases on credit.

SCHOOL WORK

At A-School there were other ratings, such as Yeoman (YN), Personnel man (PS), Disbursing Clerks (DK), Aviation Storekeepers (AK), and Religious Petty Officers (RP) in attendance for their specific training. I learned a little about those ratings, but I was prideful about being an SK. My class was made up of roughly 15 students from various backgrounds. Our instructor had a lot of energy and was always ready to teach and share her fleet experience. Lessons in class were challenging, but for the most part, it involved reading and studying after class. Moreover, I became motivated after learning that any student with the highest-grade point average by graduation would be meritoriously advanced to the rank of E-4.

I quickly set myself apart from the rest of the class by taking notes and studying after school. The rest of my peers seemed more interested in going to the mall and showing off on base. Midway through school, I became one of the top three students in class. Although I dedicated most of time studying, I did find time occasionally to enjoy my roommates. On one occasion, we took a road trip to my roommate's home in Columbus, Georgia. I got my first taste of White Castle burgers and attended a big state fair with some wild

Georgia folks. At a different time, my friends and I got our first tat-
toos in Meridian. We had good times.

Back in A-School, I had a lot of pressure to stay in the top of
the class academically. Overtime, our class began to pick sides. Un-
beknown to us, we had fan clubs and they would bet on who would
lead or drop out of the race to the top. Grades were normally posted
at the beginning and end of the class. And each point earned on
a quiz or test made the difference between dropping from number
one to five, or vice versa.

I began to isolate myself to keep away from distractions in A-
school, such as dating, parties, or hanging out for the sake of hanging out. On the day of graduation, my competition was named the
top of the class and was meritoriously advanced to the rank of Petty
Officer Third Class (E-4). I had the second-highest grade point average and was surprised to learn that I would also meritoriously advance to E-4, but only after a few months after I reported to my next
command onboard the USS HUE CITY (CG-66).

What did A-School teach me? It taught me that I had to make
sacrifices to get what I want. I sacrificed going to the mall every
weekend and hanging out late at night with friends because I
wanted the sweeter prize of becoming an E-4 with more pay and
responsibility. As my recruiter said to me in the beginning, things
were starting to fall into place.

THE MIGHTY HUE CITY

I checked onboard the USS HUE CITY (CG-66) a little more prepared than I did when I arrived at A-School. My military bearing
was in check and I felt knowledgeable about my job. I was ready to
get on the ship to show my talents. Once again, after meeting up
with some of my peers, I was told to throttle back all the high energy I had.

The ship was cold and smelled like steel. It was a smaller ship compared to an aircraft carrier, but to me, it seemed big and confusing to find my way around. I was given a top rack in the Engineering and Supply berthing. I had to meticulously climb to the top while trying to avoid stepping on anyone's rack. Did I mention it was cold in there? I was issued one itchy wool blanket to keep me warm throughout the night. To describe it in one word would be

"unbearable." I had to bundle up with extra clothing my first night on the ship.

During the next few days, I met other young Sailors on the ship and quickly learned about the ship culture. There had been a lot of turnover on the ship, so I was a part of the new wave of Sailors coming to replace those who had recently left the ship. I noticed a lot of Texans on the ship, so naturally, we gravitated around each other for support. Sailors from Georgia made up the next big demographic on the ship. Needless to say, we had lots of Texas versus Georgia comparisons on the ship.

I was never one to brag, so whenever I would mention my E-1 rank, I would get laughed at. I got the "you're at the bottom of the totem pole," or how my life was "going to be hell moving up the ranks from E-1 to E-4." All the while, I would think of how funny they would look when I would advance to outrank them in the next few months.

JAX

The HUE CITY was homeported in Mayport, a small city in Jacksonville, Florida. Sunshine and beaches were the motto. My shipmates and I would venture to the beaches to walk the strip or go to the local malls to talk to young ladies in the city. The club scene was crazy out there as a young man in the Navy. One of my shipmates was born and raised there, so whenever we went out, we received V.I.P. treatment as part of his entourage.

Jacksonville was different than Texas, but in a good way. Every weekend was an opportunity to show our excellence. We washed our cars religiously and made sure we looked good before going into town. Jacksonville kept me conscious and always aware of my surroundings.

On the ship, it was a much different story. Everything seemed routine. I woke up for breakfast, went to Quarters to hear the plan of the day, worked in my division, had lunch, got yelled at, and swept up my workspaces before being let off for the day. After a few weeks of this, I was told by my Chief whom I hardly saw, that I would be going to mess cranking for 90 days.

MESS CRANKING

Mess cranking was an assigned duty for junior Sailors to assist Culinary Specialists in the galley. Cranking duties included prepping food, cleaning the mess decks, serving food to the crew, and cleaning dishes for the crew. I went to the galley with a positive attitude. I had no idea how demanding and challenging the Culinary Specialists had it onboard the ship.

Their day started around 4 a.m. cooking breakfast for the crew. Sanitation was also a big deal in their world. Everything had to be wiped down and cleaned. If food was not prepared according to recipe cards, it had to be thrown away and redone. I was impressed to learn how the crew got their food from start to finish. With that, I worked my way up from being a dish washer to serving food on the main crew line. I even earned the reputation of serving the entire crew within 15 minutes after the mess line was open. That day, I was so fast serving food, the mess decks ran out of seating space and crew members had to eat standing up.

The one thing I hated about cranking was smelling like food every day. Also, the trash from the galley smelled horrible and it was a gamble taking it out to the dumpsters on the pier. Trash bags would either tear walking through the ship or tear on the pier right before it ended up in the dumpsters. My experience mess cranking taught me that in life there are some shitty jobs everyone must take turns doing. But hey, it built character and made me a better person going back to my division. On top of that, I was able to network and build relationships with crew members. It paid dividends when I returned to my division for work.

WORK

When I returned to work, a buddy of mine that I came to the ship with me from A-school was excelling in the division. But he was tapped to be my replacement for mess cranking duties. It took about a week or two, but I quickly established myself as one of the subject matter experts in the division. Shortly thereafter, I was advanced to E-4 (Third Class Petty Officer) as a result of my achievement in A-School. My next goal was to earn my Enlisted Surface Warfare pin on the ship and begin studying for my E-5 exam.

To earn the Enlisted Surface Warfare pin, I had to learn about the ship's history, characteristics, and capabilities. It was fascinating to learn about engineering and the ship's combat systems. I gained a better understanding on how everyone on the ship contributed to the ship's overall mission. It was hard work though. Long nights and stressful underway periods. Heck, my buddy from A-school was my study partner and we had to work around his schedule while cranking. When it was all said and done, we were the first junior Sailors with a shiny warfare pin on our chests. We set the standard for other Sailors to follow.

JB

When my buddy and I checked on the ship as Seaman Recruits, we were put under the tutelage of an E-5 supervisor nicknamed JB. He used his rank to bully us. For instance, when we got our work done, he seemed to always find something meaningless for us to do. On top of that, we would always get tasked with cleaning details sweeping or scrubbing floors. My buddy used to hate him for that. One day, JB got in trouble for using the government vehicle to move his personal belongings without proper authorization. Not only was he unauthorized to use the government vehicle, but he somehow damaged it and tried to cover it up.

Well, he got in trouble for it and got his rank reduced to an E-4. After that, things went downhill for him. Anything he did was scrutinized and wrong. He got in more trouble and ended up becoming an E-3. Meanwhile, my buddy and I were becoming superstars on the ship and quickly advanced to the rank of E-5 together. The tides shifted and Mr. JB now had to report to us for instruction.

I wasn't too tough on the man, but payback was a bitch. My buddy had the man painting decks, sweeping the floors, and doing all kinds of useless tasks. I learned from that experience to treat others how I wanted to be treated. Especially in the military, a lower rank can easily outrank a senior at any given time in the military organization.

LEADERSHIP

Over time, I became the work center supervisor in my division, which meant I was pretty much the one running the show. My buddy and I were classmates in A-school, got our surface warfare pin together, and had both made E-5 together, but now I had the top spot in the division. I started to sense negative energy whenever I gave orders. And at times, he would challenge my authority in front of the junior Sailors in the division.

It took a while for me to confront him about the issue because I did not want to ruin our friendship. But he was making me look bad in front of my Sailors. My breaking point came when I tasked my buddy to pick up some parts on the pier and he shrugged me off as if he had other important things to do. I was furious because my junior Sailors and I were hauling heavy parts from the pier to the ship and here he was telling me that he didn't have time for it. I lost my shit. I got so mad I think I was ready to fight him on the spot.

After I calmed down, I gave him a written counseling for his insubordination. We talked afterward, and I expressed how I felt and asked how he would have handled the situation if he were in my shoes. We settled our differences and had each other's back from that point on. Life was good again.

LEADERSHIP II

Time passed and we got a Master Chief to lead our division. I admired him a lot because he took time to teach and mentor. Up to that point, I had never seen anyone in the Chief ranks show that much attention to our division. I remember an instance where he was working late to balance financial records and he summoned me to his office. I thought I was in trouble, but he wanted me to watch and learn how to balance the financial report. He trained and taught me the value of learning.

Master Chief eventually transferred, and we got a Senior Chief as his replacement. Before the Master Chief transferred, he told me the new Senior Chief would look out for me and make sure that I was taken care of on the ship. However, the Senior Chief had other plans of his own. During this timeframe, the Aviation Storekeeper rate merged with the Storekeeper rate. Thus, the fleet was mixing things up by assigning AKs to SK billets and vice versa for them to learn each other's jobs. The Senior Chief was an AK who had transferred from an aircraft carrier. The way he supplied support on the aircraft carrier was different compared to supply support onboard the HUE CITY.

Shortly after he arrived, there was a First-Class Petty Officer who reported to the ship. It didn't take long for the division to figure out she transferred to the ship because the Senior Chief had asked her to follow him there. He promised to *"take care"* of her when it came to performance evaluations and accolades. I began to notice how I would be overtasked while she received all the credit. Although she lacked technical knowledge, she had great human relation skills. She was great at motivating our group when the Senior Chief had bad ideas for the division.

Since the Senior Chief lacked technical knowledge, it became difficult in the division when I needed reliable answers. After a while I just ignored him. He was a joke. Since I was considered a subject matter expert, I became one of the go-to persons to answer supply related questions. It angered him to know I knew more than he did as an E-5. Furthermore, the Senior Chief was junior to the other Senior Chiefs on the ship, so my division no longer had the support to stand up to other work centers when they were wrong. Like I said before, it made our jobs harder.

Nonetheless, I carried on my duties and set a goal to transfer without any issues. I was so fed up, I did not fight for a transfer award when my time was up to transition to my next duty station in Pensacola. Regardless of what the Senior Chief thought of me, the rest of the ship knew and respected my work ethics. I was proud to know I made my mark on the HUE CITY.

P-COLA

My new duty station in Pensacola was out of my element. I was used to working alongside a group of storekeepers. But at the new command, it was just me and another storekeeper. The rest of the sailors were of a different rating and focused on information operations.

Another downside of Pensacola was its location. It was remote and far from any real city life. For the first few weekends, I drove back to Jacksonville just to go to clubs and hang out with friends. Those were 10-hour round trips. After wasting gas and money, I decided to give Pensacola a chance to see what it had to offer.

In Pensacola, there were about two or three clubs worth going to at that time. The city was so small that once you saw people in one club, you were guaranteed to see them again in the next club and everywhere else around the city. It got annoying real quick. Not my type of scene. At work, I quickly established myself as the go-to guy. I took time to meet new people from various departments and started to get involved in activities and organizations within the command. After a few months, I became eligible to take the advancement exam for my next higher paygrade (E-6).

I studied for the exam, but when the results came out, I missed advancement by half a point (.5). Back then, when Sailors missed advancements by a point or two, commands found "award points" to make up the difference. And since I never received a transfer award from the HUE CITY, I reached back for help.

I called the ship and spoke with the First-Class Petty Officer about my dilemma and request. I could hear her in the background asking the Senior Chief about the award and his response was "I'll see what I can do." Fun fact, "I'll see what I can do" is the Navy way of saying "No". I crossed my fingers anyway and hoped for a miracle.

After a week went by, I gave up hope and decided to get back to the drawing board to study for the next exam. When the results were announced, I missed advancement. But this time it was by a fraction of a point (.02). The command was in shock, but there was nothing they could do to help.

Again, back to the drawing board.

Other Sailors were begging to study with me, but quite frankly, most of them were dumbing me down. They expected me to give them knowledge but lacked information to share or elevate me. I became a recluse and studying became second nature. On my third try, I passed the exam with extra points to spare. That experience taught me to invest in myself and not rely on people to control my destiny. It was clear the Senior Chief on the HUE CITY wanted me to fail, but I persevered through it all. God's blessings cannot be stopped.

INDIVIDUAL AUGMENTEE

With new rank and responsibility, life was getting good. However, things took a sharp turn shortly after I was promoted. I remember it like it was yesterday. It was a routine Friday, until I received a phone call to report to the Command Master Chief's office. He talked about an upcoming mission and told me I was selected to go on an Individual Augmentee (IA) assignment to Iraq. And by the way, I had two weeks to prepare for it.

I freaked out. At the time, I had an apartment and a car to worry about. More importantly, I was dating my girlfriend, who would later become my wife, and knew she wouldn't take the news well. Like any irresponsible young man, I called her best friend and told her to break it to her instead. To be honest, the IA was my call of duty, but I considered it a test on my relationship with my girlfriend. I was praying for her to stay by my side.

Two weeks came in a flash. Before I knew it, I was on a flight to San Diego, California to complete medical screenings and administrative paperwork. Afterwards, our unit got shipped out to an army base in New Jersey for combat training. Sailors in the unit came from various Navy installations. Our ranks ranged from E-1 to O-6; we even had a few Air Force and Army personnel as part of our unit.

COMBAT TRAINING

Training was intense. Most of the unit was not proficient with weapons. As a result, we received a crash course in weaponry and went straight to the shooting range for practice. We shot in the morning, afternoon, and at night. We shot when we were hungry, we shot in the cold, laying down, and in the sand. You name it, we did it while shooting.

I was no marksman, so I struggled throughout the training. As a unit, we had to pass a series of shooting ranges in order to fully complete our training. One particular range gave me serious challenges. I had to run with my rifle and shoot moving targets. If that wasn't hard enough, on the last leg I had to put on a gas mask and shoot more moving targets all within an allotted timeframe. It was tough.

I would try and fail, move to the back of the line, restock my ammunition and get ready for another shot. After day three, I was feeling defeated. My initial group kept dwindling as people passed and moved on to the next course. I had nightmares about that gun course, worrying whether I had what it took to complete it.

Like clockwork, we left the barracks to shoot at the break of dawn and returned late at night. Each time our van returned, the people in the unit would wait to see who passed and who failed. Those who passed got off the bus with smiles and enjoyed the rest of their evening celebrating with food and late-night television. On the other hand, the rest of us who failed quickly took showers and went straight to our racks to get some rest for another early start in the morning.

When I finally passed that gun range, I felt like a warrior. That day, I learned to trust my weapon and it trusted me. The rest of the gun ranges were a breeze after that. With training completed, we geared up and received our itinerary for our next mission stop. Destination: Al Asad, Iraq.

AL ASAD

The plane ride to the other side was exciting. Everyone felt motivated. After all, we had been through a lot to get to this point. We made a pit stop along the way for an in-theater brief and for more gear before we arrived at the base in Iraq. The heat in the Middle East was no joke. It felt like my face was burning off my skin when I got off the military plane. Some folks initially struggled to breathe in that environment. After a few minutes, we gathered ourselves and kept it moving.

Before we arrived in Al Asad, the U.S. Army oversaw the base. However, when my unit arrived, the base was transitioning to have the U.S. Marines take charge. The Army had been there for a while and were eager to leave. Frankly, the way they did business was without any sense of urgency, from my observation. That changed once they left and the Marines assumed command.

Marines have a way of doing things. They shoot to kill and pay attention to detail. When the Marines stood up command, everyone knew the base was not to be messed with. It was a great feeling knowing we would be well protected. However, the place took a toll on me mentally.

NANCY

While in theater, I was assigned duty as "Host Nations." Basically, when local nationals or third-country nationals wanted access to the base, they notified me to verify their credentials. Since we dealt mostly with local Iraqis, I was assigned an Iraqi interpreter named Nancy.

She was an older educated woman who was healthy and very religious. Nancy instantly took a liking towards me and treated me as if I was her son. She shared about the old good days in Iraq when there was no war and everyone looked out for each other. She studied abroad and was well known in her community. She married a European man and they had a son together. Life was simple.

When things started getting bad with Saddam Hussain in power, people started fleeing the country. Nancy remained optimistic things would get better, so she stayed. However, things got worse and country embassies began informing their countrymen to leave Iraq. Some Iraqis began to leave as well.

According to Nancy, Saddam Hussain started realizing Iraqi professors, scientists, and engineers were leaving the country, so he tracked them down and gave ultimatums. Nancy was one of those individuals Saddam gave an ultimatum. He told her if she wanted to leave out of the country, she could but had to leave within a specified timeframe. Her intuition told her to stay so she stayed.

Unfortunately, some of her colleagues who took the deal were never heard from again. Nancy's husband and son found a way to leave Iraq, but Nancy stayed and became stuck in her county. It broke my heart to learn the day she said goodbye to her family was the last time she contacted them in person.

GOOD PEOPLE

Nancy and I had casual conversations about everything. We talked about my upbringing and had thought-provoking conversations about life. One day I told her I did not know how to drive a stickshift vehicle. So the next day she got a truck, took me to an open field and taught me how to drive a stick shift. That's the kind of person Nancy was.

She introduced me to date fruits and taught me local Iraqi phrases. She even took me to a place on the base rumored to be where one of the prophets in the Bible stopped for rest. My interpreter was revered on the base. She was a wise woman and the other interpreters always gave her respect. Nancy was great!

Occasionally, she would request time alone to reflect on things. Especially when she heard of military operations happening outside of the base. It was hard for her to face the fact that her country was being destroyed with no signs of progress in sight. Unfortunately, it was a hard reality for many local nationals on the base.

For example, local Iraqis who did not reside on base had to return to their homes in the evening off base. The locals would tell me how they would be interrogated on base for information about terrorists or risk losing their privileges on base. Likewise, when they went home, locals in their community would threaten them for information about base operations or risk the lives of their family members. Those individuals struggled daily to find their moral compass.

Time flew by in Iraq. I worked out daily, ate hearty meals, earned my Fleet Marine Force warfare insignia, and even experienced a sandstorm there. We celebrated Thanksgiving, Christmas, and the New Year there. Together, we made the best of the experiences. They unified us. As I stated before, time flew by and before we knew it, our reliefs started flying into Iraq to relieve us of our duties.

Nancy took it hard when reality set in that I would be leaving Iraq soon. She took time off while I conducted my turnover. When she returned, she was very emotional and sad that I was going to be leaving her behind, but she understood. Nancy taught me a lot in the short time I spent in Iraq. I learned about the Iraqi culture, the people, and how the war changed the Iraqi way of living. The news media only painted a one-sided view of Iraq. However, Nancy woke me up to what was really happening in her country. She taught me to value everyday relationships and I was grateful to learn from her. She was truly good people.

TIME TO ROTATE

After we completed our turnovers, we received our itineraries and left on a flight back home. We all felt accomplished in our own unique way. During the flight, the attendants gave us all alcoholic beverages and kept thanking us for our service. Furthermore, when we landed stateside, people were greeting us and shaking our hands as we were connecting to our various flights.

In Pensacola, I was surprised to see my immediate family and girlfriend waiting for me at the airport. I had lost some weight from working out, so my mother kept trying to feed me at every available opportunity. After a weekend of family time and satisfying my food cravings, I went back to work to catch up on things. Things hadn't changed much, but I was informed that I was in my window to start negotiating for transfer orders to a new duty station.

Since I had completed a tour in Iraq, I was supposed to receive orders of my choice. But that was not the case. I wanted to go to a ship in Jacksonville, Florida, but according to the detailer, he did not have anything available. After a few days of discussing options, the detailer told me that his best option was for me to be assigned to a precommissioning unit. I had no idea what a pre-commissioning unit even meant. But in true Navy fashion, the detailer told me to either take the orders or be assigned wherever he saw fit. I took those orders.

T-AKE 5

The pre-commissioning unit was called the USNS ROBERT E. PEARY (T-AKE 5) and she was in its final build stage in San Diego, California. The ship was scheduled for a homeport shift to Norfolk, Virginia after completion. San Diego reminded me of Florida; the weather was perfect, and people were carefree. I was met at the airport by another Sailor and he took me to where the ship was docked.

On the way, he spoke about the new ship and how we would be the ones setting the baseline. The ship had a small military detachment, while the rest of the crew was made up of civilian mariners. The senior military officer was called the OIC (officer in charge) and there was a junior officer we called the AOIC (assistant officer in charge). On the enlisted side, there was a Chief Petty Officer, three FirstClass Petty Officers, four Second Class Petty Officers, and two Third Class Petty Officers. We were a small-knit crew. One of the First-Class Petty Officers was a lady named M who outranked the rest of us, based on seniority. However, I was put in charge as the Leading Petty Officer (LPO) because the Chief felt I was more assertive when it came to giving orders. I embraced the new responsibility.

As a group, we were diverse. One Sailor had an aviation background, while another came from the submariner community. We even had a Sailor who had experience working with the Seabees. Collectively, we shared ideas and came up with best practices as a team.

We joked a lot and had a great time exploring San Diego and the surrounding areas. On the base, I would go around to various ships to get ideas on how to implement training and programs on the PEARY. On one occasion, I visited the PEARY's sister ship named the USNS SACAJEWIA to inquire about their programs. To my surprise, I was greeted by one of my A-School classmates! She was my competition back in A-School and was the number one student in the class. Professionally, she had beat me again.

She was wearing a khaki uniform, which meant she had promoted to the rank of Chief Petty Officer (E-7). I was proud of her accomplishment. She jokingly told me I was slacking and better be in khakis the next time she saw me. It motivated me. We talked about her road to success and how she got her pre-commissioned ship ready for sea. I took her advice and set up our programs with her blueprints. When it came time to set sail, our crew was set up for success and ready to support the fleet.

BOARD

The ship's first mission was to replenish ships in the South America theater with a follow-on objective to shift to our homeport in Norfolk. South America was a blast. The ship visited Panama, Curacao, and Djibouti. While deployed, I took the Chief's exam for the first time, passed and became board eligible. Being board eligible meant my service record would be reviewed by a board of Master Chief Petty Officers. After review, they would determine if I was worthy for selection to the rank of E-7. It was a big deal. M also made board, so we made a pact to help each other out and not change on each other if one of us made it and the other didn't. Things were on track. Deployment was smooth, and we made it safely to our new homeport in Norfolk.

DRAMA

While in Virginia, we scheduled meetings with Master Chiefs and other Chiefs to give us recommendations about our records. M had a brother in the Navy who had recently made Chief, so she invited me to speak with him about his process. Our meeting went well. Before I left, her brother extended the invitation for me to bring my record over for review. Well, my record had already been reviewed by Master Chiefs and Senior Chiefs. And quite frankly, I was to the point where I felt it was too late for me to make any more changes in my record. Thus, I declined his request.

At the time, we were getting ready to set sail for another deployment, so the preparations also kept me busy. Thus, I submitted my Chief package and waited for the results. However, once the deployment started, M's demeanor towards me changed.

I would discuss plans or ask for her input on ideas and would get blank expressions from her. If that wasn't enough, she made jokes about my leadership style around the other Sailors. But when I would come around, she wouldn't say anything and tried to avoid me. It got to a point where I asked the Chief to mediate between us so we could at least appear unified in front of our enlisted crew. It only worked for a day or two.

I reached my breaking point when she made a smart comment towards me in front of others. The Chief brought us together again and told us to figure it out. As we were talking things out, she revealed the reason she shunned me was because she felt I disrespected her brother by not showing him my record before I submitted it to the Chief's board. I almost laughed in her face, but I held my composure because she was actually being serious about what she was saying. My initial thought process went something like this: First of all, it was my damn record and if I didn't want her brother to see it, that was my right. Secondly, I knew for a fact her brother wasn't upset at me because he never gave me that indication. Lastly, there was absolutely nothing her brother could have done to make my record better. He would have made a few comments, but ultimately, I had to figure it out on my own. Thus, I saw no real benefit in meeting with him.

Those months of worrying about what I had done to negatively impact M was a waste of my time and energy. I learned from that experience to follow my gut and not let the perceptions of others affect my stress levels. A few weeks later, I received an encrypted email from the Military Sealift Commander. The email read, "Congratulations on your selection to SKC"- I made Chief!

TRUST THE PROCESS

I was in shock. Shortly after, I received another email from a friend of mine named Bryan who was also on deployment, but on another ship. He had also been selected for Chief. Since both of us were part of the Military Sealift Command, we were instructed to fly back to Norfolk to participate in the Chief's initiation process.

Bryan and I had a unique bond. We both enlisted and advanced in rank around the same timeframe. So, it was fitting when we got selected for Chief at the same time. I also emailed my classmate from A-School to let her know that I made it. She congratulated me and told me she was selected for an officer program. Once again, she was a step ahead of me. I told her I would catch up, but for now, I was focused on making it through the initiation process.

Deployment in the Navy is a time to save money, selfreflect, and workout to get in shape physically. Bryan and I were on two separate ships, but we had dedicated ourselves to the P90X program. When we returned back to Norfolk, we were in the best shape of our lives. However, it seemed like the other Chief selectees stationed on shore duty were not on the same physical fitness program. From our perspective, the physical portion was going to be a joke to us.

For the record, hazing is no longer part of the Chief's initiation process. Wherever the Chiefs would have normally hazed, they substituted that phase with strenuous physical activity. To Bryan and me, the physical activity was a typical P90X session. We would do the workouts with ease and yell smart comments such as, "Give me more" or "Is that all you got?!" It was hilarious. Our fellow selectees hated us for it.

We would always rebuttal with, "We just came from a deployment serving our country, what did you all do?" They would throttle back and politely ask us to tone it down so the beatings could stop. Those were some of the best times of my Chief selectee experience.

I was a hard knock Chief selectee. I once kicked out a Genuine Chief from our selectee meeting because I felt he was being an idiot. He was surprised that I was being serious. He pouted, but he left from our meeting. Our group of selectees went through a rigorous phase and together we learned how to trust each other and function as a team. It was a hard journey, but we made it through our hell night. On September 15, I put on my khakis and was pinned with my earned Gold Fouled Anchors.

CHIEF

Life as a Chief was great! Bryan and I were a force to be reckoned with. We would walk around the base and correct Sailors for minor uniform infractions. In the Chief's Mess, we have a saying, "The Chief is always right." With my khakis on, no one challenged me except other Chiefs or senior officers. Back then, I considered officers with the rank of lieutenant and below as not my equals. As far as I was concerned, they were too junior in the Navy to provide valuable input, unless they had a prior-enlisted experience. I did not salute those individuals.

Around the base, I would meet Master Chiefs and they would acknowledge me by saying, "Oh, you're Bonsu? You were highly recommended during the board. They say you get things done and don't take any shit. Welcome to the Mess." It was a great compliment to know members in the senior enlisted community valued my work ethic.

Back on the ship, it was business as usual. But it seemed like I was getting an upgrade on everything. I had to change my room and was even eating in a different dining facility with more food options. I also had more access to people and resources. As the Chief, I no longer had to get my hands dirty with technical intricacies of work because that was the responsibility of the First-Class Petty Officers. However, I needed to avoid being idle. Thus, when I had downtime, I would visit other ships on the piers to see if I could share my technical expertise. I enjoyed meeting other enlisted storekeepers and providing mentorship. Since I was a young Chief, the junior Sailors gravitated around me and wanted to know about my career path.

While visiting ships, I saw a frigate on the pier and stopped by to assist the storekeepers. Through conversation, I learned they had been without a Supply Chief for over a year, and their department head was running their division. It piqued my interest. I went on board, introduced myself to the Supply Officer and asked if I could look over her supply records. She was grateful, but I was amazed by how screwed up the records and operations had been.

With the First-Class Petty Officers on the PEARY running operations, I made plans to return to the ship for a couple of hours a week to provide training to get the storekeepers back on track. We started with basic customer service, record keeping, and accountability for received material. By the end of the week, the storekeepers were operating two times better than they had the week before. The Supply Officer was also impressed and asked me to stay longer. I declined her offer.

Although it seemed challenging, I had never been on a ship that small before and was unsure if I wanted that stress and headache. A week later, I received a call from the Regional Commander. Apparently, the Supply Officer called to complain about her Chief vacancy and specifically asked for me to fill that void. There was no way around it, I was going to be transferring early from the PEARY to the HAWES.

HAWES

I checked onboard the USS HAWES with mixed emotions. The ship was not my ideal place to serve in my new Chief role, but I knew I could make a difference in the Supply Department. On a frigate, the Supply Chief oversees all the supply divisions. That meant I would be in charge of four divisions: S-1 (Stores), S-2 (Food Service), S-3 (Ship Store), and S-4 (Disbursing).

The Food Service division had a bunch of junior Sailors who did not want to be in the Navy. A lack of leadership and poor morale had tainted their outlook of the Navy. The division was led by a First-Class Petty Officer and SecondClass Petty Officer who had recently reported to the ship. The Second-Class Petty Officer had aircraft carrier experience and was very structured. He was all about military bearing and doing things by the books.

Similarly, the First-Class Petty Officer was an aircraft carrier Sailor. He was used to having an abundance of Culinary Specialists around him to make things in the galley run smoothly. However, on the HAWES we lacked the resources and personnel to run our galley efficiently. At any rate, the junior Culinary Specialists aboard HAWES hated those two. The junior Sailors would argue and put forth minimum effort. At times, it seemed as if the two new Culinary Specialists had to beg the juniors to perform their jobs. It was UNSAT (unsatisfactory); not what I wanted to see in my Navy.

S-3 & S-4

The Ship Store division was in charge of laundry, the barbershop, vending machines, and a mini mart on the ship. The division sort of ran itself, but they lacked leadership. There was a First-Class Petty Officer in charge, but he was nearing retirement. Nothing was a priority for him. He would brush off major issues as though it would get fixed on its own. A young E-4 was really in charge of the division. He would occasionally ask the First-Class Petty Officer to speak on his behalf to get his point across.

Disbursing on the ship runs like a bank. At the Disbursing Office, Sailors could cash checks and conduct money transactions. A junior Supply Corps Officer operated the Disbursing Office aboard the HAWES. However, his division fell under my purview, so I received most of the ship complaints regarding his services.

In a nutshell, those were my four main divisions I had to get back on track. To complicate things, there was a major upcoming supply inspection in a few months. I had to get on my grind.

GETTING STARTED

I first got acquainted with each of my Sailors to better understand their professional goals. Next, I laid out my expectations and told them that I would be very transparent with them. As usual, the ship's constant underway schedule was a contributing factor on the negative morale. The crew hardly had breaks for themselves. As a result, it was causing personal issues with their families and social lives. Further, the lack of resources and personnel put a strain of them mentally and physically.

For instance, my first underway with the ship was full of complaints about the lack of supply resources. Some Sailors would complain about their meal portions. If that wasn't the complaint, then it was about the food and its lack of taste. The Culinary Specialists could have cared less. They would argue with the crew and stop cooking if they felt offended about any little thing. And that was just the food part; my galley was dirty and unsanitary. To top things off, their record-keeping needed a major overhaul. Needless to say, working with the Culinary Specialists was my top priority.

GRIND

I was no expert on the S-2 division, so I requested assistance from the Fleet Assist Team for an honest assessment of our operations. When the team arrived, they weren't as shocked as I thought they would be. The team got straight to business and gave me helpful tips to improve my division.

They even took time to mentor and train the Culinary Specialists.

During training, there was a big focus was on sanitation. The Fleet Assist Team found dirt and scum in unimaginable spaces. They also found expired and rotten food in freezers that were supposed to be emptied and cleaned daily. I was embarrassed for my Culinary Specialists, but it gave me a point of reference to verify and inspect their work from that point on.

Next, they taught the Culinary Specialists how to be creative with their meals. We even came up with challenges and empowered the Culinary Specialists to take turns being supervisors in the galley. They enjoyed that. The SecondClass Petty Officer was a known records keeper from his previous command, so the team offered to work with him to get our records back to par.

Aside from that, my other obstacle was to get them focused at work and manage their distractions outside the ship. Working with those Sailors in the galley taught me patience and how to listen. Once I listened, I was able to adjust my leadership style to meet their needs, which in turn allowed them to put forth their best efforts.

S-1

The Stores division was my bread and butter, so it broke my heart to see the operations in shambles. I conducted a sample inventory to get a feel for inventory accuracy; the S1 team scored 40%. Mistakes I found included parts mislabeled, incorrect counts, and parts in the wrong locations. It was a hot mess. My First-Class Petty Officer at the time was trying his best, but he also lacked some basic rate knowledge. I made a point to train him and the team as much as possible.

In that division, we had a Sailor from Russia. He was one of my best Sailors to work with. Whenever I gave him a task, he would find a way to streamline it to make it better. He was educated and was working on his Ph.D. at the time. But he had a thick accent and some of the crew members would make fun of him because they could not understand him. The First-Class Petty Officer and I had to constantly defend him from the crew.

Another challenge I faced was that he took everything I said literally. For instance, if I cussed somebody out for being an idiot, he would make them an enemy until I said otherwise. However, the one thing I admired about him was his work ethic and his honesty. Whenever he would make a mistake and I got angry, I would yell, "What the f*&^, why did you do... (so and so)?" He would say in a humble manner, "Chief, I do not know how to do this. Can you show me?" Ordinarily, Sailors would make up some stupid excuse about why they did a stupid thing. But this Sailor told me every time when he did not know something. With that, I had no choice but to cool down and provide him with the job training he needed. I truly admired him for that.

DISBURSING

The Disbursing Officer ran a one-man show. Since he was an officer, I gave him some latitude to conduct his business. Now and again, someone would have an issue and I would relay it to him to make corrections. All things considered, we had a good working relationship. On one occasion, I corrected him about some minor issue, and he made a comment that he outranked me, so he didn't have to listen to what I had to say. Well, I was not about to have a junior officer talk crazy to me as the Chief (at least not on my watch). So I checked him and I continued with my daily business.

However, when I went into the Chief's Mess to take a break, I was met by the Senior Enlisted Advisor and he "wanted to talk". In short, the junior Supply Officer went to him to complain that I disrespected him. I brushed off the Senior Chief's comments, but when I saw he was seriously questioning me, it lit a fire in me and I began to get defensive. We exchanged words and I felt some type of way being questioned by a fellow Chief who was supposed to have my back. In the end he agreed with me, but then he said, "Well, technically he outranks you, so you should be more careful."

That pissed me off! It was at that moment that I knew I had to make a transition to become an officer in the United States Navy. If my voice was not to be heard and respected as a Chief, then I was in the wrong business, Jack.

FRIGATE LIFE

Life aboard the frigate was rough. We came to work before dawn and left work when it was dark outside. Due to the ship's small size, we knew everyone on board and had to rely on each other to make the ship function properly. I miss that comradery. We got through inspections together and supported each other during underway periods. So, when we found out the ship would soon decommission, we pulled together to send her off the right way.

To this day, I have the highest respect for any Sailor who served on board a frigate. It was by far, one of the most challenging moments in my career professionally. I endured so much stress and pressure to make the HAWES Supply department great. Luckily, my wife and I were in separate states at the time. My long working hours and compounding stress could have been a recipe for divorce or turmoil in our relationship. However, we persevered through it all. That experience made me a better leader and strengthened my faith in God.

STA-21

Before I reported aboard the HAWES, I submitted an officer package through the Seaman to Admiral (STA-21) program with the support from mentors and leadership aboard the PEARY. STA-21 is an enlisted to officer commissioning program that offers paid tuition to a college or university with an approved Navy ROTC program on campus. I initially applied for the officer program before I was selected for Chief. When the genuine Chiefs found out, my road to Chief became more intense.

Nonetheless, I wasn't selected during that period (I thought I was a sure pick). Well, I was selected as an alternate. Which meant I could only proceed if someone declined their selection or got medically disqualified. None of which happened. I was briefly discouraged, but was uplifted by mentors to tighten up my package and resubmit it. I took their advice. And just as the HAWES was getting ready to decommission, it was announced throughout the ship that I had been selected to become a Supply Corps Officer under the STA-21 program. My next hurdle would be finding a university to attend and making it through the Naval Science Institute (NSI- a mini boot camp for officer candidates).

NSI

I arrived at Newport, Rhode Island for NSI during the winter. The weather was brutal. I was quickly humbled when I saw my peers selected for the program. Our ranks ranged from E-1 up to E-8. We quickly formed and normed to ensure we made it out of NSI together.

A Marine Gunnery Sergeant and a Senior Chief oversaw our group. But after a few days, they pulled us together and told us we could manage ourselves since we all had prior fleet experience. With our experience and skillsets, we made sure all our administrative, medical, physical, and education requirements were met. For example, we had Seal team members who helped our group stay in shape physically. Likewise, when it came to academics, we had junior Sailors from the nuclear community who taught us how to better understand subjects such as thermal dynamics and engineering.

At NSI, we did everything together. It strengthened our commitment to become impactful Naval officers. The experience was humbling. The lesson I learned at NSI was to value everyone, regardless of rank. We helped each other get through that process. With that, as a group we completed our stop at NSI and departed to our designated universities. My next stop would be Prairie View A&M University in Texas.

PVAMU

Going to Prairie View A&M University was the best academic decision I've made to date. I love my HBCU! What drew me to the school was the level of professionalism from the staff and the determination of the students. In class, our dialogue was always open and thought-provoking. We were taught to think outside the box and to become change agents.

As an older student, I was never isolated. Everyone treated me equally. However, being an older student had its challenges. I recall being in class taking handwritten notes on trigonometry, while my peers were playing games and taking pictures on their phones. I was thinking, "These guys are crazy and not serious about their education." I finally asked a student why the class lacked interest. The student informed me that trigonometry was a subject taught early on during high school. Also, taking pictures of the notes with their phones was much easier than writing it on paper.

With that in mind, I had to catch up with technology, academically, and socially. The tutoring labs became my secondary home. There, I learned trigonometry, calculus, and physics. I even took tutoring lessons to improve my writing skills. I was never shy about asking for help.

ROTC

In addition to my classroom studies, I was a part of the Navy ROTC program on campus. With the ROTC midshipmen we conducted military drills and keep current with military trainings. As an enlisted Chief, I was asked to mentor and provide my fleet experience as an added perspective. The midshipmen at Prairie View were great. They were highly motivated about being future officers and warfighters.

We had study sessions and group workouts to push each other academically and physically. I remember a midshipman in one of my calculus classes, and he was super smart. He asked me one day if he would be a good officer based on his level of calculus knowledge. I told him, "That doesn't mean sh*t! You might know calculus, but I know Sailors. That's what counts."

I majored in Business Management and was one of the top students in the College of Business that year. I earned my commission in 2013; Ready to get back in the game to support the fleet!

NAVY SUPPLY CORPS SCHOOL

My first stop after my commission was back to Newport for Navy Supply Corps School. We were a big group of students, so we were divided into two class groups, Alpha and Bravo. I was in the Alpha class. Some of my classmates had professional experience in business, information technology, and education. Others played collegiate sports, and some were also prior enlisted. In class, we learned the business side of Supply Management, Disbursing, Food Service, and Ship Services.

The highlight of Supply Corps School was the orders reading event to determine our job assignments. It was setup as if we were getting selected for the NBA draft. When my name came up for selection, the USS KEARSARGE (LHD-3) was displayed on a big screen. Some students congratulated me, while others looked disturbed. A disturbed classmate later told me he had a friend on the ship and heard it was a terrible ship. He even told me he felt sorry for me. My response was classic. I told him, "So you're telling me that ship is terrible, huh? Well, that's great! I'll be a superstar there. If they are already at a zero, anything I do right will be phenomenal. That's my kind of ship!"

KEARSARGE

When I checked aboard the KEARSARGE, it was dry docked going through a maintenance phase. The ship was away from its homeport in Norfolk, Virginia. I checked onboard the ship quickly and my sponsor got me up to speed with the ship's operational tempo. After the maintenance phase, it was rumored there would be a major inspection called INSURV to certify the ship for deployment.

Nonetheless, the officer I was to relieve wasted no time with our turnover. During turnover, he would say things such as, "Oh, that is not a big deal. Don't worry about it." But I knew better; he wanted to turn his mess over quickly to shift accountability on me. I didn't have much to work with, but I assumed duties as the Wardroom Officer as my first division officer role.

As the Wardroom Officer, I was in charge of Culinary Specialists and Food Service Attendants who maintained officer spaces known as the wardroom. My division was also responsible for cleanliness and maintenance of all those spaces. Right away, I identified the main issue in the division: There was a lack of skilled workers. Traditionally, talented Culinary Specialists and Food Service Attendants work in the wardroom. Yet, I had to fight tooth and nail to get quality Culinary Specialists and Food Service Attendants to work for me on the ship.

After I finally got my crew together, we got right to business by fixing discrepancies. For example, the officer bathrooms were unsanitary, so we did a deep clean and even painted the bathrooms. Also, some staterooms had bunks with missing lights, mattresses, pillows, and chairs. Each stateroom seemed to have its issue, and I owned over a hundred of them.

Furthermore, I was in charge of collecting mess bills from officers for the meals they consumed on the ship. Believe it or not, officers on the KEARSARGE were cheap when it came time to pay their mess bills. I made personal visits to each officer to collect those dues as if I was the tax collector. After a while, they got the picture. Some officers started paying their mess bills months in advance to avoid my visits. Those were fun times...

Remember when I mentioned earlier about that INSURV inspection? Well, the ship had a few months to prepare for it. During that inspection, every space, division, and program gets reviewed and evaluated. After a few selfassessments from the Supply Department, it was identified that the ship's Hazardous Material (HAZMAT) Division required a commissioned officer to be in charge per instruction. Thus, I was tasked to also take charge of the HAZMAT Division.

HAZMAT

There was a seasoned Chief running the HAZMAT division at the time. The initial plan was for me to be the "division officer" on paper while the Chief continued to operate the division. I was a bit skeptical about the idea since my name would be on the line. So, I decided to review their records and observe the operations for my peace of mind. I'm glad I did, because HAZMAT was all jacked up and needed a major overhaul.

There was HAZMAT unaccounted for, improperly labeled, and the shelf-life program was poorly managed. When I questioned the Chief, he would get defensive and say, "Well, no one has complained about it." My thought was, "No s*@#. No one knows any better." To complicate matters, the junior Sailors couldn't stand the Chief. They felt overworked because the Chief wouldn't listen to their ideas to improve the workload. It was either "Chief's way or the highway."

As the new ranking officer, I gave the Sailors freedom to try new things as long as we reached the same goals. The Chief did not like my way of doing things, but I countered his concerns with "If it's wrong, I will take the hit" or "My name is on the line anyway. I got it." We clashed a lot. But in the end, my way of thinking paid dividends when it came time for our INSURV inspection. Both of my divisions passed without any issues. Lessons learned during that experience were to trust my gut feeling and avoid the status quo.

I felt like the subject matter expert in both of my divisions. Thus, I requested to transfer to a different Supply division to learn something new. But when I asked for the transfer, I was told my knowledge and experience in the wardroom was invaluable. It took three months of persistence before my request was granted. Becoming the Disbursing Officer would be my next challenge.

TURNOVER

Like my predecessor, I was eager to conduct turnover. Unlike my previous experiences, I planned to turnover a well-organized division. My relief was robotic and timid. He was good with policy and procedures. But he lacked the ability to connect with the enlisted Sailors. For whatever reason, he could not grasp that concept. We did a formal turnover and I made sure he had all the resources he needed to be successful.

My new position as the Disbursing Officer was very important. I oversaw large sums of money and was accountable for Navy Cash equipment around the ship. I had a Disbursing Deputy who helped as my assistant. She trained me on everything disbursing related and how to be a good Disbursing Officer. We worked well as a team.

All the while, the ship was going through a series of sea trials and inspections to certify the ship for deployment. We deployed later that fall.

CRUISING

It was busy leading up to deployment. The ship had not deployed for some years, so everything seemed foreign to the crew. We also embarked Marines for the deployment; they were everywhere. Marines were either working out in the gyms or congregated on the mess decks waiting for the meal hour to begin. Some Sailors aboard felt the Marines were a nuisance and always in the way. But I enjoyed their company because they enhanced our fighting capabilities.

During the deployment, I had three other roommates in my stateroom. My roommates were the ship's Repair Officer, Intel Officer, and the previous Disbursing Officer whom I relieved. There was always laughter in our stateroom. Working out in the gym was something that we all had in common. So whenever possible, we aligned our schedules to work out as a group. The start of deployment was epic! Well, until we made a port stop in Dubai...

STUDY YOUR FRIENDS

When the ship pulled into Dubai, the entire crew was anxious to get off the ship. We completed our daily duties quickly and paired up with our liberty buddies to explore the town. There was a "Wardroom hail and farewell" planned that evening to welcome new officers and celebrate those leaving. My buddies and I made note to stop by there later that evening.

After exploring the town with friends, we finally made it to the wardroom function. Drinks were flowing and everyone was having a good time. At a certain point, it started getting late, so my friends and I got ready to return to the ship. When the duty van arrived to start taking officers back to the ship, I was one of the first to volunteer for a ride back.

As we loaded the van, I noticed my roommate (prior Disbursing Officer) in the van, so I went to greet him. After I was seated in the van, I leaned forward and put my hand around him to ask about the event. He abruptly pushed my hands away. Since we had been working out on the ship, I thought he was challenging me to show off his strength. Challenge accepted!

Thus, I started to flex and wrestle him to submit to my will. He started to flex as well, and I honestly couldn't tell if we were playing or fighting. Either way, I wasn't about to lose.

After a few seconds, someone yelled for us to cut it out, so we stopped. Since I thought we were playing, I thought nothing of it. The van returned to the pier and I got off to hang out with my other roommate for a brief period. When the drinks at the wardroom function started catching up with me, my roommate and I got back on the ship. I went straight to my bed to sleep it off.

MORNING AFTER

In the morning, as all my thoughts were coming back to me, I remembered the incident with my roommate. But before I could find the right time and place to apologize to him, I was called into the Executive Officer's (XO) Office. I was in shock, more so that the incident in the van reached that level of attention at the command. After speaking with the XO, I was told I would have to speak with the CO later regarding the issue. In the meantime, I had to sign a protective order to stay away from my roommate. It felt like I was being treated as a criminal.

I replayed the van incident in my mind repeatedly, trying to figure out what went wrong. Nonetheless, I felt terrible about the situation and kept thinking if I had left him alone, none of this would have happened. I even tried to rationalize it. Maybe he was upset about something and I was the trigger. The incident happened on Christmas Eve. Being on deployment away from family and friends can take its toll. Maybe that was it.

The next day, I went to see the Captain (CO) to explain what happened. I made a mistake, owned it, and wanted to make it right. The CO looked at me and said he didn't believe me and thought I was hazing my roommate. He went on to say due to the incident, he did not want me working in Disbursing. I was crushed. All I could do was break down and cry.

Furthermore, I had to sign additional paperwork stating that my actions were inappropriate and if it happened again, a negative entry would be annotated in my service record. Looking back, the paperwork was just a slap on the wrist, but it was scary and embarrassing going through that process. From that point forward, I wasn't the same on the ship. I could hardly eat or sleep. I also lost my motivation to get up for work or exercise anymore. The incident made me realize everyone wasn't my friend, especially not my former roommate.

CHANGES

For the record, my roommate and I were both liked on the ship. But when the incident happened, it made people choose sides. Some were calling my roommate a snitch, while others said I was too aggressive in dealing with him at the time of the incident. However, the consensus was that my punishment was too harsh. As a wardroom, we were supposed to handle things at the lowest level and take care of each other. But it seemed like most had turned their backs on me.

Following orders, I turned over my job to a newly reported Supply Corps Officer. Super cool guy. Patient, understanding, and a good listener. He helped me get through my situation more than he knows. It is crazy how a listening ear can ease a stressful moment. Although I was sad leaving my job, I was glad to give it up to a standup guy.

After I finished the turnover, the SUPPO and I went to see the CO again to plead my case. Again, I apologized and asked for the opportunity to apologize to my roommate in person. The CO declined my request and said he thought it was not an isolated incident. I was crushed once again. Later that evening, the SUPPO called me into his stateroom and asked if I would consider leaving the ship earlier than my normal transfer date. I thought it was some sort of trick question, but he was serious. He didn't see any positive outcomes if I stayed on the ship.

The SUPPO called my detailer and after a few minutes, he handed me the phone. To my surprise, my detailer was my previous AOIC when I was stationed on the USNS PEARY. He was encouraging and supportive. He even shared that he went through a similar situation during his division officer tour. He learned from it, picked his head up and moved forward. He understood my predicament and was willing to work with me. During that moment, I felt blessed and highly favored. A week later, I received new transfer orders and departed the ship shortly thereafter. My initial orders were to report to Sigonella, Italy for my next assignment.

NEW BEGINNINGS

Before the deployment, my wife gave birth to our third child Cameron, who had some breathing complications after birth. Well, as we were planning our move, my son got sick and had to spend some time in the hospital for treatment. When the physician found out we were scheduled to travel overseas, he deemed my son unsuitable to travel. He said the medical staff in Italy did not have the specialized equipment needed to treat my son if he got sick again. As a result, I had to decide whether to keep my orders or cancel them to stay with my family. After careful consideration, I chose family. My detailer worked the order modification and I was reassigned to Aviation Support Detachment (ASD) Oceana in Virginia Beach.

ASD Oceana was a breath of fresh air. And for once, I could hear myself think. When I arrived, the command was preparing for an inspection called SMA (Supply Management Assessment). I quickly plugged in and became the new guy with fresh new perspectives about their programs and policies. ASD Oceana would become a new challenge later down the line. But for now, it was a new beginning to reset my gears and be the best Supply Officer I could be.

REFLECTIONS

My tours have been challenging, with unique obstacles along the way. The journey is not over, and I am navigating through challenges as we speak. When asked about my fondest memories, without fail, I would tell you it was meeting my wife in Pensacola and the birth of our children. Without their support, I really don't know how I could carry on defending our country's freedoms.

I also miss the calm of the seas, comradery, and all the wonderful people I have met along the way. It brings me comfort knowing that I served as a role model for some in our military organization. Moreover, if you should take anything away from my story, know that there is always victory after adversity. Some victories happen sooner than others do, but the way forward is to face them head-on and keep the faith. Lastly, do not let your struggles define you or compromise your goals. Stay the course and keep grinding.